W9-AAD-119

Dora's Time to Shine

Aurora Colón García
Illustrated by Becky Radtke

Rigby®

A Harcourt Achieve Imprint

www.Rigby.com
1-800-531-5015

Literacy by Design Leveled Readers: *Dora's Time to Shine*

ISBN-13: 978-1-4189-3907-6
ISBN-10:   1-4189-3907-2

© 2008 Harcourt Achieve Inc.

All rights reserved. No part of the material protected by this copyright may be reproduced or utilized in any form or by any means, in whole or in part, without permission in writing from the copyright owner. Requests for permission should be mailed to: Paralegal Department, 6277 Sea Harbor Drive, Orlando, FL 32887.

Rigby is a trademark of Harcourt Achieve Inc.

Printed in China
1 2 3 4 5 6 7 8 985 13 12 11 10 09 08 07 06

Contents

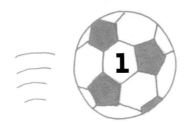

The City Tournament

Weaving in and out among members of the opposing team, Dora dribbled the soccer ball and kicked it to Daisy. Daisy moved it closer to the goal and then, with one smooth kick, passed it back to Dora, who sent it sailing into the net. The Tornadoes' fans were especially excited because their team was playing a great game in the city tournament, in which all the schools in the area gathered to play against each other.

The players left the field just long enough to catch their breath and position themselves for the kickoff.

"We're playing like a couple of World Cup champions!" Dora whispered to Daisy as they lined up on the field.

Dora shook her hands to relax, took a running start, and then kicked the ball down the field. A player from the opposing team stole the ball and ran toward the goal while the fans chanted, "Go, Norma!" She moved the ball easily up the field, her head held high. Norma, an expert at handling the ball and setting up her teammates to score, was clearly the leader of her team.

Daisy ran next to Norma, trying desperately to recover the ball for her team, but Norma changed directions. She skillfully managed to keep the ball away from the other team's players in spite of their efforts to steal it back. The Tornadoes, discouraged because they couldn't stop her, seemed to move out of her way.

"Don't give up!" shouted Dora as Daisy attempted to stop Norma. With a quick move of her leg, Norma changed the direction of the ball and continued up the field. Without warning, the ball flew past the goalkeeper.

The first half of the game ended in a tie, and the roar of the crowd echoed like the rumble of thunder as the players quickly ran off the field.

"Norma may be a skillful player, but all of you are just as good," Coach Alba reminded the Tornadoes. "Try your very best and don't give up!"

"I'll do my best!" Dora whispered to herself as she dribbled the ball toward the goal at the start of the second half. Glancing sideways, Dora noticed Norma coming up behind her, swinging her foot forward to steal the ball. When Dora attempted to block her move, the two players became tangled, lost their balance, and tumbled to the ground.

"Foul!" yelled the official, holding up a yellow card and running toward where Dora and Norma were lying in a heap on the ground.

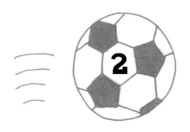

The Injury

Norma bounced up instantly and extended her hand to Dora.

"Are you OK?" she asked with concern in her voice.

Dora closed her eyes and tried to catch her breath. As she carefully tried to stand up, Dora groaned in pain, her legs folding beneath her.

As the official signaled a time-out, Coach Alba ran out on the field to assist Dora. Supported by Coach, Dora was able to limp off the field.

Dora's ankle throbbed with pain as she struggled to hold back her tears.

"Everything will be OK," Coach Alba promised Dora as she put an ice pack on Dora's ankle to prevent swelling.

Mom and Dad, who had been watching the game from the stands set up on the sidelines, hurried over to the edge of the field where Dora was resting.

Mom hugged Dora immediately, and Dad asked, "Are you all right, *Mijita?*"

"My ankle hurts!" she exclaimed, pointing to her bruised, swollen ankle.

"I think you should take Dora to the doctor to make sure that nothing is broken," urged Coach Alba.

"I'm all right, Coach," said Dora, trying to hide her pain. "Please, I want to stay here until the game is over."

"*Mijita,* let's make sure that you're okay and nothing is broken," said Dad.

"Don't worry, Dora. We'll all do our best to win the game just for you," promised Daisy. Dora could only nod her head as Dad carried her off to the car. Because Dora's ankle was turning purple from the bruising, Dad feared that her injury might be serious. He knew how much this game meant to Dora, but he also knew that it was important to have her ankle checked.

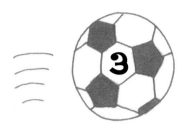

At the Clinic

With Dad's help, Dora limped up the sidewalk, through the door, and into the waiting room at the clinic. She grew more and more nervous as she waited for her turn to see the doctor. She secretly worried that her injury was so serious that she would never play her favorite sport again.

"I don't think your ankle is broken, Dora, but let's take some X-rays just to make sure," Dr. Ruiz said kindly.

Mom, aware that her daughter was in pain, tried to cheer Dora up with a soccer magazine that was lying on the table in the waiting room.

"Look, Dora, Dr. Ruiz must be a soccer fan, too. This magazine is all about the World Cup."

Paging through the magazine, Dora couldn't take her eyes off the story and photos of the World Cup games.

As she read about soccer champions from around the world, Dora began to think about what it would be like to play on a World Cup team. "Why don't women play on the World Cup teams?" she wondered. "How often do World Cup players practice, and what kinds of injuries do *they* suffer? Could I ever play on a championship team?"

Lost in the article, Dora almost forgot that the results of her X-rays would determine whether she could play for the rest of the season.

Dora's heart raced excitedly as she imagined what it would be like to play in huge stadiums all over the world.

Dora slowly paged through the photos that showed her favorite soccer heroes in action, and suddenly she became Dora Cruz, World Cup soccer player! The roar of thousands of cheering fans, anxious for the game to get underway, rang in Dora's ears. . . .

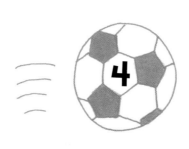

World Cup Champions!

This was a proud day for the Tornadoes, chosen to represent the United States in one of the most important sports events of the year.

Looking around the immense stadium, Dora realized that a nine-year-old girl had never played in a World Cup championship match before. Suddenly she was on the field, the familiar feel of the freshly cut grass beneath her feet.

Dora looked to her right, and there on the field next to her was Daisy, smiling confidently at her. Dora skillfully kicked the ball around the opposing players and out of their reach, before they even realized that she was near. She smoothly made her way toward the net, darting around the quick opposing team players. Her foot connected with the ball, which sailed past the surprised goalkeeper and into the net.

"The Tornadoes score!" the announcer shouted into the microphone as the crowd went wild. "Dora Cruz is having an amazing game, and the Tornadoes are trailing by only one point."

Dora looked up into the crowd and caught a glimpse of her family in the stands—Mom and Dad proudly waving American flags, while Grandpa and Grandma cheered. Omar did a little dance and yelled, "Way to go, U.S.A.!"

All around the stadium, fans were dressed in red, white, and blue. Dora felt so proud to be representing the United States.

Quickly Dora returned her attention to the game as her team kicked the ball. When she looked at the opposing team, the players seemed frozen, and Dora effortlessly took control of the ball. With her powerful kick, Dora sent the ball flying swiftly over the goalkeeper's head and into the goal.

The fans were wild with excitement as the announcer described Dora's amazing play in detail. With Dora's last-minute goal, the Tornadoes had tied the World Cup game with a score of 2–2, sending the match into overtime.

"You're doing a great job, team," praised Coach Alba. "Try your best during overtime and have fun!"

The stadium shook with energy as the fans stomped and screamed. Because the score was still tied after the extra period of play, the outcome would be decided by a shoot-out. Each coach selected five players who would take turns trying to score a goal for their team. The team scoring the most goals in the shoot-out would be the winner.

Coach Alba picked Daisy, Eliza, Madison, Fatima, and Dora to represent the Tornadoes.

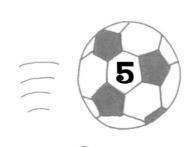

The Shoot-out

The shrill sound of the official's whistle signaled the time for the shoot-out to begin. The fans in the stadium were silent as the five kickers chosen from each team lined up. Sweat rolled down Dora's back as the team captains got ready for the coin toss. "Heads," she called out as the official flipped the coin, but the coin landed on tails, so the opposing team kicked first.

Dora developed a game plan, imagining how she would move the opposing players from place to place on the field like checkers. She knew that she could score easily if she used all of her skills.

Both the crowd and the players grew anxious as the opposing team got ready to kick. The first player took a running start, sending the ball flying with one smooth, strong kick. Right on target, the ball landed between the goal posts, and the score was now 3–2.

The Tornadoes went next, and Daisy (the first to kick for her team) felt the pressure. The fans were so quiet that Daisy could hear her heart beating in her chest. As her good friend got ready, Dora thought to herself, "You can do it, Daisy."

Confidently, Daisy dribbled, aimed, and made contact with the ball.

Daisy could barely believe how hard she had kicked the ball, which sailed high over the goal. She trotted off the field, her head lowered, disappointed that she wasn't able to help her team.

"It's OK, Daisy, you tried your best!" Dora comforted her.

The excitement rose as the teams took turns kicking the ball toward the goal. Finally with the score tied at 4–4, the championship came down to the last pair of players.

As the final player from the opposing team prepared to kick, Dora closed her eyes, hoping that the ball would miss the net. The opposing player kicked the ball out of bounds and slowly jogged over to the sidelines.

The outcome of the game now rested with Dora, the last player to participate in the shoot-out. Nervously shaking her hands, she stepped up and carefully positioned herself for the short kick. Dora effortlessly lifted the ball with her foot, scoring the winning goal.

Players and fans alike celebrated wildly as the Tornadoes won their first World Cup! Dora's teammates captured her in a single huge embrace, then raised her high up on their shoulders. . . .

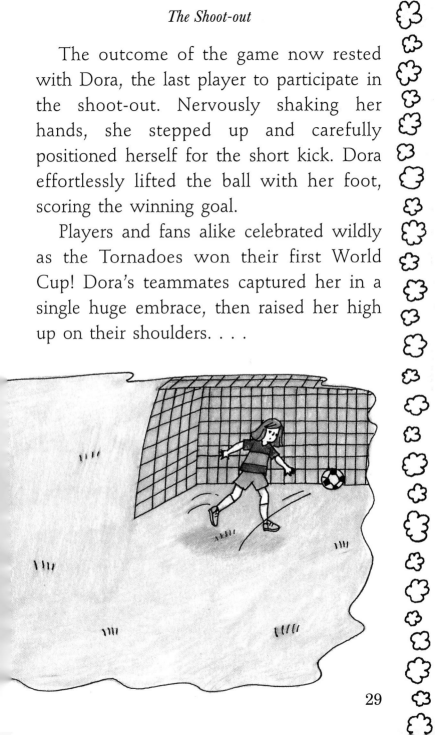

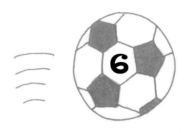

The Good News

"Dora, we won!" Daisy exclaimed as she burst into the waiting area at the clinic with her parents, causing Dora to look up from the magazine.

"I know! We won the World Cup!" replied Dora, still starry-eyed.

"What are you talking about?" asked Daisy, confused. "Are you sure you didn't hit your head?"

Dora suddenly realized where she was and that Daisy was talking about the city tournament.

"No, I'm OK," Dora smiled. "We're waiting for the X-ray results."

"You have nothing to worry about," announced Dr. Ruiz as she returned. "You twisted your ankle, but it will heal quickly if you rest for a week and wear this brace to strengthen it."

Since Dora had thought it would take longer for her ankle to heal, one week sounded like music to her ears. She wouldn't be able to run or play at soccer practice, but she could sit by the sidelines and support her teammates. "Dad, just wait until Coach Alba hears the good news," said Dora.

As Dora's injury healed, Daisy helped Dora with her ankle exercises. Daisy encouraged Dora every day by telling her, "You're doing so well that I just know you're going to be able to play in the State Finals on Saturday."

"I hope so," Dora replied. "I really want to play in the finals!"

"Dora, what if we lose in the finals?" asked Daisy. "That last team we played was tough to beat, and it will probably only get tougher."

"Everyone on our team is a great player, and we'll do our very best. We'll play like they do in the World Cup soccer games—with lots of spirit and lots of skill. Remember our favorite chant from the games: *Sí se puede.* . . . Yes, we can!" Dora said.

Dora's memories of her own trip to the World Cup gave her confidence in herself and in her team.

"*Sí se puede,*" said Daisy.

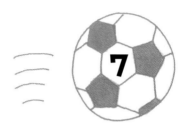

The State Play-offs

The day of the State Finals arrived, and Dora joined her teammates on the field, ready for the kickoff. Although she was wearing her brace from Dr. Ruiz, she worried that her ankle might fail her during the game.

The game began, and the Tornadoes were ready. Daisy took control of the ball and dribbled it to Eliza, who moved it down the field. Skillfully the Tornadoes passed the ball from one player to another. When the other team got too close to Daisy, she kicked the ball to Dora, and Dora continued toward the goal.

Dora didn't look nervous, but she could feel her entire body trembling as she dribbled closer and closer to the goal and attempted to score.

Because she was afraid of hurting her ankle, she kicked the ball gently, and it rolled only a few feet. She knew that her team was depending on her and didn't want to let them down.

"That's okay, Dora, you'll get it next time!" yelled Daisy, trying to comfort her.

The opposing team also had an opportunity to score, but they missed, as both teams did a great job defending their goals.

The score was still 0–0 when the official signaled the two-minute warning. Everyone felt the excitement in the air as players on both sides scrambled for the ball. Coach Alba called a time-out so that Dora could adjust her ankle support. The team needed Dora to be strong in this game. Ready to give it her best, Dora was determined to play like a World Cup champion—with confidence and skill.

Back on the field, the opposing team dribbled the ball toward the goal, and suddenly Daisy appeared out of nowhere. She stole the ball from the opposing team player, changed directions, and passed it to Dora.

As Dora moved the ball down the field, she could hear someone chanting, *"Sí se puede,* Dora!" Recognizing her and Daisy's favorite World Cup chant, Dora began to feel confident and strong.

Dora looked up into the stands and saw Omar and Carlos proudly chanting, *"Sí se puede!"* Grandma and Grandpa joined in the chanting, and Mom and Dad did the same. Soon spectators throughout the whole stadium were chanting, *"Sí se puede!"*

Dora dribbled the ball down the field, skillfully passing it back and forth to her teammates. *"Sí se puede!"* drifted across the field as she approached the net.

The opposing team guarded Dora closely because they expected her to attempt the goal, but she had a plan. Instead of kicking the ball toward the goal, she changed directions and passed it to Daisy. Daisy kicked the ball back to Dora, thinking Dora was going to score. But again Dora passed the ball to Daisy, and Daisy swiftly kicked her foot forward, connecting with the ball.

With just seconds left in the game, Daisy's ball hit its mark, and the Tornadoes won by a score of 1–0. Loud cheers rocked the stadium, and the entire team rushed to surround Daisy and Dora, while their families beamed with pride.

In a special ceremony, the gold cup was awarded to the new state champs. Coach Alba announced that Dora had been named MVP (Most Valuable Player) for the tournament because Dora had set up the great play that won the game.

Dora accepted the award humbly, thanking all of her teammates for their efforts. "I would like to share this award with Daisy because without her we couldn't have won this championship!"

"Thanks, Dora," said Daisy. "*Sí se puede!*"